100 Things

you should know about

Samurai

100 Things

you should know about

Samurai

John Malam

Consultant: Fiona Macdonald

MASON CREST PUBLISHERS INC.
370 Reed Road
Broomall, Pennsylvania 19008
(866)MCP-BOOK (toll free)
www.masoncrest.com

ISBN: 978-1-4222-1973-7
Series ISBN (15 titles): 978-1-4222-1964-5

First Printing
9 8 7 6 5 4 3 2 1

Cataloging-in-Publication Data on file with the Library of Congress.
Printed in the U.S.A.

First published in 2010 by Miles Kelly Publishing Ltd
Harding's Barn, Bardfield End Green, Thaxted, Essex, CM6 3PX, UK

Editorial Director Belinda Gallagher
Art Director Jo Brewer
Assistant Editor Claire Philip
Volume Designer Simon Lee
Image Manager Liberty Newton
Indexer Gill Lee
Production Manager Elizabeth Collins
Reprographics Stephan Davis, Ian Paulyn

ACKNOWLEDGEMENTS
The publishers would like to thank the following artists who have contributed to this book:
Julian Baker (J B Illustrations), James Field (Beehive Illustration), Mike Foster (Maltings Partnership),
Oliver Frey (Temple Rogers), Andrea Morandi, Nick Spender, Mike White (Temple Rogers)
Cover artwork: Mariusz Kozik
All other artworks are from the Miles Kelly Artwork Bank

The publishers would like to thank the following sources for the use of their photographs:
t = top, b = bottom, c = centre, l = left, r = right
Alamy Page 9 Mary Evans Picture Library; 14 Photos 12; 21 V&A Images; 33(r) Interfoto;
40–41 Photos 12; 46(c) Tibor Bognar
The Art Archive Page 11(t) Rijksmuseum voor Volkenkunde Leiden (Leyden)/Gianni Dagli Orti;
23(b) Bibliothèque des Arts Décoratifs Paris/Gianni Dagli Orti; 27(b); 29(t) and (c) Gunshots;
44–45(b) British Museum; 46(t) Private Collection/Granger Collection
Corbis Pages 16; 19(t); 20(b) Asian Art & Archaeology, Inc.; 44(t) Sakamoto Photo Research Laboratory
Getty Images Page 42(t) Hiroshi Higuchi
The Kobal Collection Pages 2–3; 47(b) Warner Bros./The Kobal Collection/James, David
Photolibrary Pages 17(c); 19(b) JTB Photo; 34(c) Corbis
Topfoto.co.uk Page 45(t) Print Collector/HIP

All other photographs are from: Digital Stock, Digital Vision, PhotoDisc

Every effort has been made to acknowledge the source and copyright holder of each picture.

Contents

Warriors of Japan

1 **For hundreds of years, there was a group of warriors in Japan known as samurai.** Their name means "someone who serves." All samurai served a warlord (military leader) and battles were fought between armies of rival warlords. Samurai followed a set of rules called *bushido*. These rules told them how to behave, not just in battle, but in everyday life. Respected members of Japanese society, the bravest and fiercest samurai became well-known figures.

▼ Samurai armies fought at close range, on foot and on horseback. This scene shows the Battle of Kawanakajima in 1561, in the north of the main Japanese island of Honshu.

From emperor to shogun

2 **Japan is an island country in the Pacific Ocean, located off the coast of mainland Asia.** It is made up of four main islands (Hokkaido, Honshu, Shikoku and Kyushu) and nearly 4,000 smaller ones. The islands are mountainous, with forested slopes and fast-flowing rivers. There are many active volcanoes, including the famous Mount Fuji.

◀ Jimmu, the first in a long line of emperors who ruled Japan.

KYUSHU

SHIKOKU

Osaka

Kyoto

Nara

Tokyo

▲ Japan is a nation of many islands that lie close together. It has had several capital cities over the years.

QUIZ

1. Which family took power away from the emperor?

2. Who was the first emperor of Japan?

3. What is the name of Japan's most famous volcano?

4. Which was the first permanent capital of Japan?

Answers:
1. The Fujiwara family
2. Jimmu 3. Mount Fuji 4. Nara

3 **Japan was once ruled by emperors.** Legend says that the first emperor was Jimmu, who reigned in 660 BCE. Early emperors had great power. Then, in about 800 CE, they became "figurehead rulers." This meant that they were still heads of state, but had little power.

HOKKAIDO

HONSHU

itachi

► Japanese history is divided into several periods. These are often named after the most powerful family, or the site of the capital city at that time.

DATE	PERIOD	NOTABLE EVENTS
14,000–300 BCE	Jomon	• Early people are hunter-gatherers and decorate clay pottery with distinctive patterns
300 BCE–300 CE	Yayoi	• Farmers begin to grow rice in paddy fields
300 CE–710	Kofun	• Buddhism is introduced to Japan
710 CE–794	Nara	• Nara becomes the first permanent capital city
794–1185	Heian	• Kyoto becomes the capital city
1185–1333	Kamakura	• Battle of Dan-no-Ura • Minamoto Yoritomo becomes the first shogun
1333–1573	Muromachi	• Members of Ashikaga family become shoguns. They are finally driven out by the warlord Oda Nobunaga
1573–1603	Azuchi-Momoyama	• Oda Nobunaga is succeeded by Toyotomi Hideyoshie • Japan is reunited
1603–1868	Edo	• Japan isolates itself from the rest of the world • U.S. Commodore Matthew Perry forces the Japanese government to open up ports for trade
1868–1912	Meiji	• Japan becomes modernized and grows to be a world power

4 In about 800 CE, power was taken from the emperor. It fell into the hands of the Fujiwara clan. They were a noble family that had married into royalty, and for about 300 years they were the real rulers of Japan. However, in the 1100s, the Fujiwaras lost control after a bitter war. From then on, power passed to military dictators called shoguns.

6 Japan's first permanent capital city was Nara, on the island of Honshu. It became capital in 710 CE and the emperor lived there. In 794 CE, Kyoto was made the new capital and home of the emperor. Tokyo, which was known as Edo until 1868, is the present-day capital.

5 Shogun means "commander of the forces." He was a military dictator—the person in control with unlimited power. In 1192, Minamoto Yoritomo became the first shogun. He was known as the "barbarian-conquering great general."

► Minamoto Yoritomo, the first shogun. Shoguns controlled Japan until 1867.

Religion and ritual

7 **Japanese society was divided between rich and poor.** A few rich families owned all the land and the poor owned none. The poorest people worked on the land, and had to pay taxes to the powerful landowners. This type of system is known as feudalism. Japan was a feudal society for hundreds of years.

▶ At the top of Japanese society was the emperor, even though he had no real power. Merchants were the lowest class.

Figurehead
Emperor
Shogun (Political leader)
Daimyos (Warlords)
Samurai (Warriors)
Ronin (Paid soldiers)
Warrior class
Peasants (Farmers and fishermen)
90 percent of the population
Artisans (Craftspeople)
Merchants (Sales people)
Lowest class

▶ There are many statues of Buddha in Japan. This one is made of bronze and is 800 years old.

8 **The two main Japanese religions are Shinto and Buddhism.** Shinto is an ancient religion in which the emperor is said to be a descendant of the Sun god. Its followers believe that spirits inhabit trees, waterfalls and other natural things. Buddhism is founded on the teachings of Siddhartha Gautama. He was called the Buddha and lived in India in the 4th or 5th century BCE.

◀ Shinto priests bang drums during ceremonies. The sound is believed to attract the gods' attention.

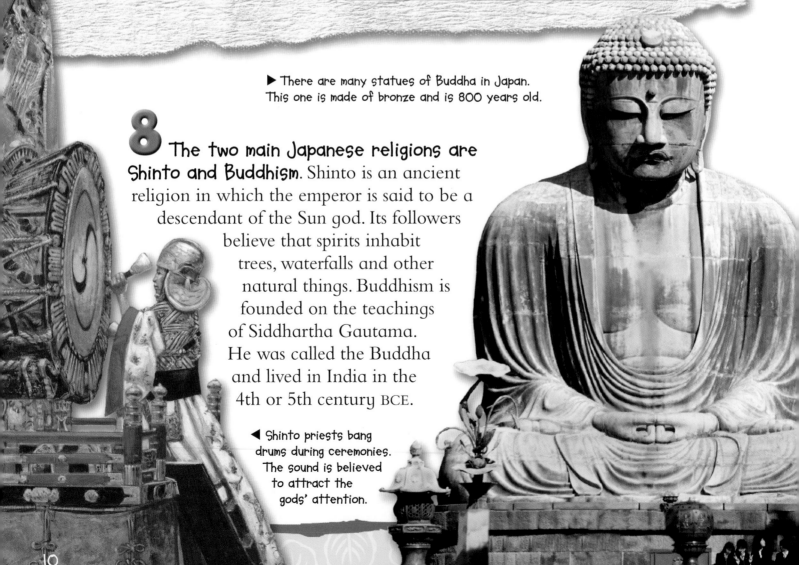

10

Before battle, a samurai warrior might visit a Shinto shrine. A priest would give him a small cup of *sake* (rice wine) to drink, and the soldier would offer prayers to a god. In return for his prayers, the soldier hoped the god would protect him. Samurai had favorite gods to pray to, such as Taira Masakado (see pages 16–17). After he died, in 940 CE, he was believed to have become a god.

◄ Shinto shrines were important places of worship. Samurai visited them to pray for good fortune.

9

Ancestors were special. If a samurai had heroes among his ancestors, he showed them respect by displaying their names at his family altar. It was a way of keeping their memories alive, and the warrior hoped he would inherit their bravery and courage.

11

Rituals were very important. These were set ways of doing ordinary things. During the 1400s, samurai began to carry out the tea ceremony. This was an elaborate way of making and enjoying a cup of tea. The tea was made by carrying out steps in a precise order.

Kama (iron pot used to heat the water)

Hishaku (water ladle)

Mizusashi (container containing cold water)

Chashaku (tea scoop)

Chasen (bamboo whisk)

Chaki (dry tea leaf container)

Chawan (tea bowl, used for drinking)

The first samurai

12 **The first samurai appeared in the 900s CE.** They were warriors who belonged to the private armies of Japan's noble families, or clans. The clans owned large amounts of land, which they needed to protect from rivals. The best way to do that was to build up an army of soldiers in case of battle.

13 **Samurai protected their bodies with armor.** The first samurai wore armor made from small iron or leather scales, laced together with silk or leather cords. The scales were arranged into separate sections, each of which was designed to protect a different part of the samurai's body.

14 **In the early years of the samurai, the soldier on horseback was the elite warrior.** He was an archer, and fired arrows from a bow as his horse galloped along quickly. The mounted archer practiced his archery techniques over and over again. In battle, when he had fired all his arrows, an archer fought with a sword.

Bow

Armored sleeve

Shin guard

▶ A samurai warrior of the 900s CE. Mounted warriors were especially skilled at using the bow and arrow.

Shoulder guard

Arrows

Armored kilt

Sword

15 Infantry (foot soldiers) were lower class fighters. It was their job to hold up their shields to protect the mounted archers, who were seen as the main fighting force. As well as defending the horsemen, the infantry were also responsible for disrupting the enemy by setting fire to their property.

Minamoto clan mon, a flower

▲ ▶ Each clan had its own *mon*, or family crest. It was used on flags, and helped soldiers to identify their comrades.

Taira clan *mon*, a butterfly

16 The two leading clans were the Minamoto (also called the Genji) and the Taira (also called the Heike). They were bitter rivals whose armies fought battles against each other to decide which was the leading clan.

Let battle begin!

▼ Battles began with archers firing a volley of whistling arrows.

17 **An argument between rival clans would often lead to a battle.** When the two sides faced each other on the battlefield, the armies followed a strict sequence of events. The battle began with archers firing arrows that made a whistling sound. The noise was believed to be a sign to the gods, asking them to protect the samurai who were about to fight. It was also a scary sound for the enemy.

18 **It was an honor to be first into battle.** A man was chosen from among the mounted warriors. He was picked because he was a champion fighter and came from a long line of warriors. Facing the enemy, he named his ancestors and listed his achievements in battle. It was a challenge to the other side to send out a warrior of equal status.

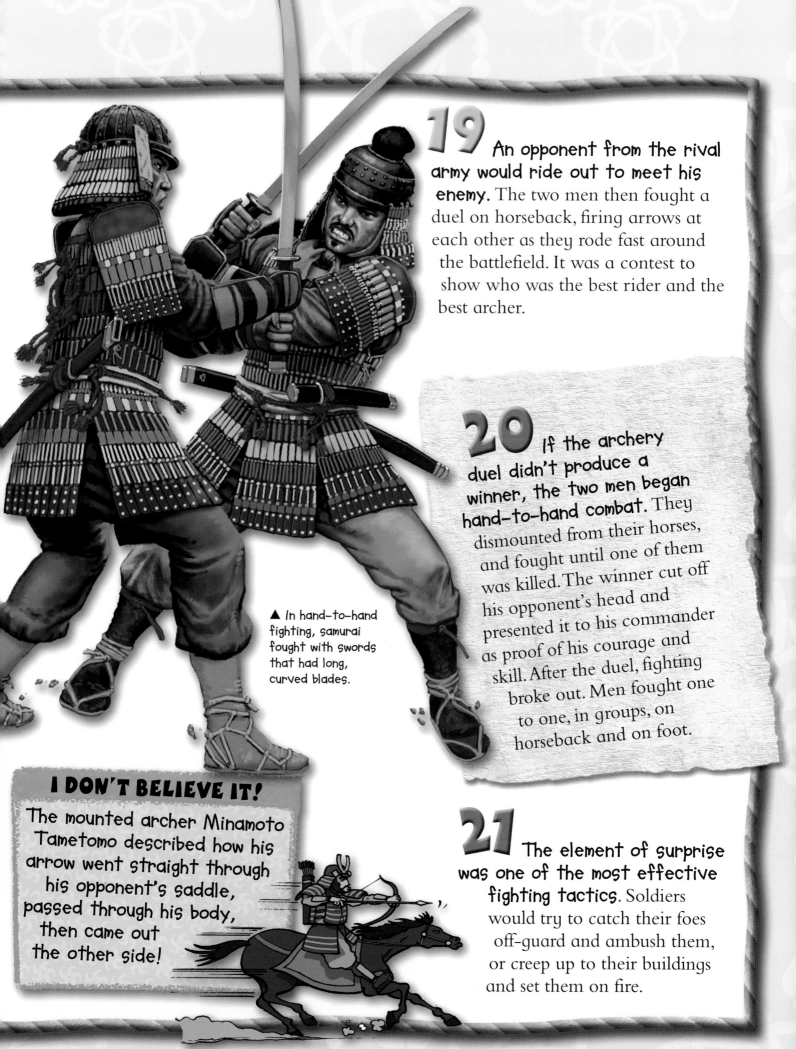

19 An opponent from the rival army would ride out to meet his enemy. The two men then fought a duel on horseback, firing arrows at each other as they rode fast around the battlefield. It was a contest to show who was the best rider and the best archer.

▲ In hand-to-hand fighting, samurai fought with swords that had long, curved blades.

20 If the archery duel didn't produce a winner, the two men began hand-to-hand combat. They dismounted from their horses, and fought until one of them was killed. The winner cut off his opponent's head and presented it to his commander as proof of his courage and skill. After the duel, fighting broke out. Men fought one to one, in groups, on horseback and on foot.

I DON'T BELIEVE IT!

The mounted archer Minamoto Tametomo described how his arrow went straight through his opponent's saddle, passed through his body, then came out the other side!

21 The element of surprise was one of the most effective fighting tactics. Soldiers would try to catch their foes off-guard and ambush them, or creep up to their buildings and set them on fire.

Taira Masakado

22 **Born around 903 CE, Taira Masakado is the first samurai commander that historians know much about.** Part of the Taira clan, Masakado was the great-great grandson of Emperor Kammu. In his youth, he served at the court of the Fujiwara clan in the capital Kyoto. The Fujiwaras were Japan's rulers at the time.

23 **The Taira clan had its origins in 825 CE, when the surname Taira was given to a branch of the royal family.** The Taira settled in Hitachi, a district northwest of present-day Tokyo. They became the ruling family of the region, and built up a private army.

24 **Masakado wanted the Fujiwaras to appoint him as head of the national police.** The Fujiwara clan refused to do this, so Masakado left their court and moved to the Kanto district of central Japan. From there, he led a war against the Fujiwara clan. In 939 CE, he conquered districts in eastern Japan and proclaimed himself as the new emperor.

▼ Taira Masakado knocks a foot soldier to the ground. In old pictures such as this, he is always shown as a brave warrior.

25

The government sent an army to defeat Masakado, who they regarded as a rebel. This army was led by Taira Sadamori. The two sides clashed at the Battle of Kojima, in 940 CE, and Masakado was killed in the fighting. His head was cut off and sent to the emperor in Kyoto as proof of his death.

▼ The Battle of Kojima took place during a gale. Wooden shields erected by Masakado's army were blown down.

26

In Kyoto, Masakado's head was put on a platform. Legend says the head flew back to Masakado's base in Kanto. From there it went to Shibasaki, where it was buried with honor. Today, that place is known as Masakado Kubizuka (the Hill of Masakado's Head), in Tokyo. Masakado is seen as a hero who fought the government for the rights of ordinary people.

▼ At the Hill of Masakado's Head, there is a shrine in honor of Taira Masakado.

Minamoto Yoshiie

27 The Minamoto clan was an offshoot of the Japanese royal family. But in the 800s CE, it was decided that none of them would be emperor. They were given the surname Minamoto and moved from the capital at Kyoto to a new base at Osaka, in southern Japan. Here they became the district's ruling family.

28 Minamoto Yoshiie was a samurai commander. He turned the Minamoto clan into a major fighting force. Born in 1039, at Kawachi, in the district of Osaka, his father was a samurai leader, and Yoshiie learned all the skills of the warrior from him.

◄ Minamoto Yoshiie was one of the greatest samurai commanders.

▶ Yoshiie earned the title *Hachiman-Taro*, meaning "son of the god of war."

29

Yoshiie's first battles were against the Abe clan. He fought alongside his father to defeat them in a war that raged for about nine years, and ended in 1062. The Minamoto clan took control of much of north Japan, with Yoshiie as ruler. Twenty years later, he defeated the Kiyowara clan, who had started to challenge him. The Minamotos were the undisputed rulers of north Japan.

I DON'T BELIEVE IT!

Once, Yoshiie guessed that his enemy was about to ambush him in a surprise attack because he saw a flock of geese suddenly fly out of a forest.

30

After each battle, Yoshiie spoke to his troops. Men who had shown the most courage were invited to sit on a "bravery" seat. All of them wanted this honor. None wanted to sit on the other "cowardice" seat. To be called a coward was a disgrace.

▼ A bronze statue of Minamoto Yoshiie in Fukushima, on the island of Honshu.

31

Yoshiie's victories made him the greatest general in Japan. He made Kyoto his home, and he hoped the government would reward him with a position of power, but they never did. Yoshiie spent his last years living quietly in the capital, where he died in 1106.

The Gempei War

32 **As Japan's clans became stronger, a power struggle began.** The greatest conflict was between the Taira and Minamoto clans, who clashed in a series of battles known as the Gempei War, fought between 1180 and 1185. Both clans were related to Japan's royal family, and they wanted to control it—and the rest of Japan.

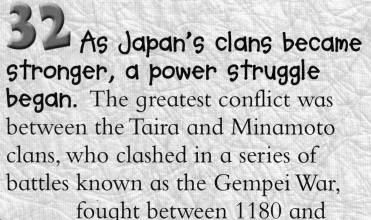

33 **The Gempei War began when Taira Kiyomori ordered the death of Minamoto Yoritomo.** Kiyomori and Yoritomo were the leaders of their respective clans. At first, the Taira forces were successful, and Yoritomo's army was heavily defeated. But the war was not over.

▶ Minamoto Yoritomo (1147–1199) led the Minamoto clan during the Gempei War.

▼ In 1180, Minamoto Yoritomo sent one of his men to kill an enemy from the Taira clan. It marked the start of the Gempei War.

34 **The Taira clan had a reputation for being harsh.** As the war progressed, Taira troops started to defect and join the Minamoto army. It was now the Minamoto's turn for battle honors. In 1183, the Minamoto army seized the capital at Kyoto, then attacked the last strongholds of Taira resistance, which were in western Japan.

SAMURAI SYMBOLS

Every samurai clan had its own *mon* (see page 13). This was a symbol that was easy to recognize. *Mons* were usually based on plants or simple patterns made from dots, curves and lines. Some were based on animals, but these were less common. What *mon* would you design for your family? Look at the *mons* in the pictures in this book to give you some ideas.

36 **By 1192, the Minamoto clan controlled Japan.** That year, Minamoto Yoritomo visited the emperor in Kyoto. The emperor appointed him as the first shogun (military dictator). From then on, Japan had two rulers—the god-like emperor (who had little power) and the shogun, the most powerful person in the land. It was a system that lasted until the mid–1800s.

▼ The Taira clan were defeated at the Battle of Dan-no-ura. This scene shows Taira Tomomori tied to an anchor, about to drown himself.

35 **The final action of the Gempei War was the sea battle of Dan-no-ura, in 1185.** Warships of the Taira and Minamoto clans fought in the narrow strip of water between the islands of Honshu and Kyushu. When it was clear the Minamoto would win, many of the Taira threw themselves into the sea.

Bushido—the samurai code

37 **Samurai followed a code of behavior known as *bushido*.** It means "the way of the warrior." *Bushido* was a set of rules that governed all aspects of a samurai's lifestyle. It demonstrated that a samurai was an educated and refined man with knowledge of the arts and literature—as well as being a brutal killer who would slice off his enemy's head without hesitation.

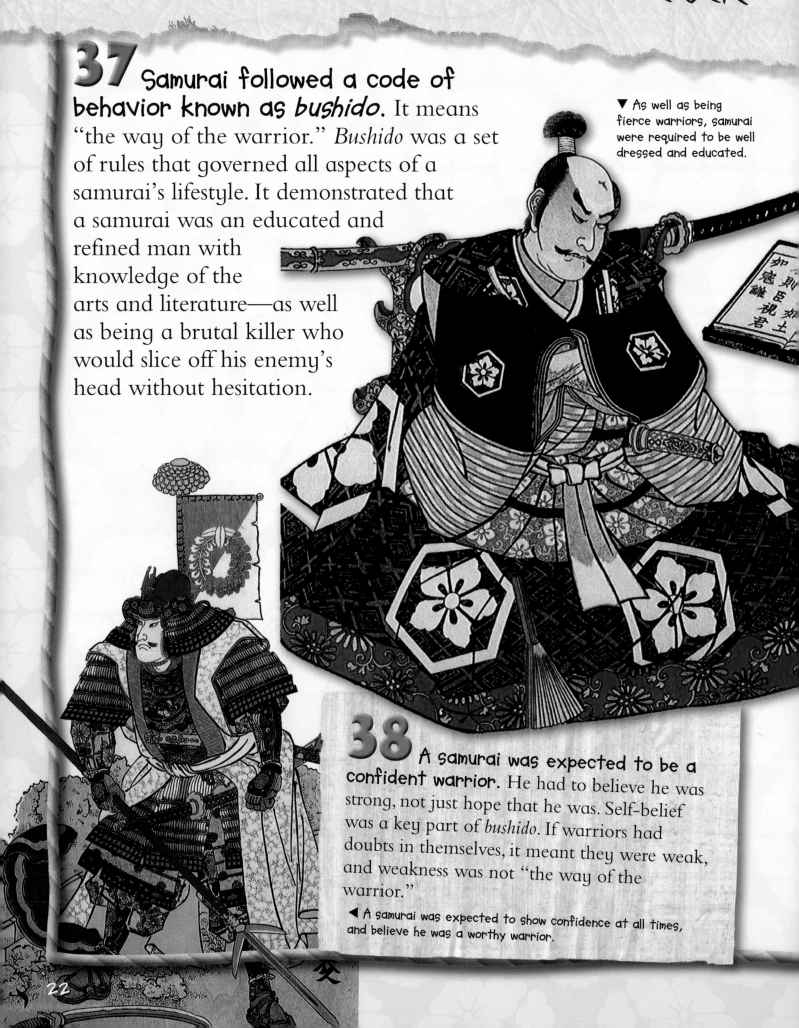

▼ As well as being fierce warriors, samurai were required to be well dressed and educated.

38 **A samurai was expected to be a confident warrior.** He had to believe he was strong, not just hope that he was. Self-belief was a key part of *bushido*. If warriors had doubts in themselves, it meant they were weak, and weakness was not "the way of the warrior."

◄ A samurai was expected to show confidence at all times, and believe he was a worthy warrior.

◄ This samurai is bowing to his master, showing he is loyal and obedient, a key part of *bushido*.

40 Courage was one of the most important rules of *bushido*. To show courage, a samurai had to demonstrate that he was prepared to fight to the death. If he was outnumbered in battle, he had to carry on fighting. Running away was a sign of cowardice, which was punished.

39 Showing loyalty to the warlord was another rule of *bushido*. The warlord gave orders, and samurai obeyed them without question. By obeying orders, samurai showed obedience.

I DON'T BELIEVE IT!

Samurai were told to be careful when chasing their enemies. If an enemy got too far ahead, he could easily turn around and charge, putting the attacking samurai in danger.

41 If a samurai made a big mistake, he was punished under the rules of *bushido*. In the most serious cases, he would kill himself. This was called *seppuku*, or *hara-kiri*. The samurai first ate a meal. After this he opened up his robes and plunged a dagger into his stomach. As he did this, another samurai cut his head off with a swing of his sword.

◄ A samurai about to commit *seppuku*, cutting open his own stomach.

Samurai armies

42 By the 1550s, Japan was divided into many states, each of which was ruled by a *daimyo*. He was the warlord and head of a clan. Rival clans were almost constantly at war with each other. To protect their territory, warlords had large armies. As fighting increased, the armies grew more organized.

43 Armies clashed during the fighting season, which lasted from spring until the end of summer. No fighting took place during the harvest season, which began in September, or in winter. Most foot soldiers were peasants from farming communities, and when it was harvest time they returned to their homes to gather crops.

44 Foot soldiers were called *ashigaru*. They made up a large part of a warlord's army, and there were always many more *ashigaru* than mounted samurai. *Ashigaru* fought with swords, spears, bows and *naginata* (see page 29). In the 1540s, they began to use guns called arquebuses.

45 A samurai army was divided into units of men. The elite troops were always the men on horseback. The *ashigaru* were organized into groups of spearmen, archers and arquebusiers (soldiers with firearms). Other groups of *ashigaru* carried flags and banners, and some were given the job of carrying the army's baggage.

46 On the battlefield, generals controlled troop movements by waving fans. The fans had swinging tassels on them, making the fan movements easy to see. Sound signals were another way of sending information to the troops, such as blowing on conch shells and beating on drums and gongs.

▼ A samurai army on the march. *Ashigaru* foot soldiers are flanked by mounted samurai. The most powerful clans had armies of over 100,000 men.

47 Boys were taught to be warriors.

They began school at about the age of seven, and for the next five or six years were taught to read, write and play musical instruments. From about the age of ten, they were taught to fight. When a boy reached 13, he had a coming-of-age ceremony, and from then on he was ready to fight in battle.

▶ Boys were taught to fight using sticks, but these would eventually be replaced with swords.

48 Some clans set up military training schools, or *dojo*. Here, boys were taught martial arts by trainers, or *sensei*. The *sensei* were skilled in the use of weapons, and had served in samurai armies. It was their job to pass these essential skills on.

49 Mounted warriors were the elite troops of a warlord's army.

Their main weapon was the bow, and they had to fire arrows at moving targets as their horses raced at great speed. They practiced by firing arrows at running dogs. At the start of training, most arrows missed, but eventually they would learn when to release an arrow to hit a moving target.

I DON'T BELIEVE IT!

Left-handed children born to samurai families had their left arms tied up, forcing them to become right-handed.

51 Women married to samurai were trained to fight. Although their main work was to look after the family, there was always a chance that an enemy raiding party might attack the family home. To fight off attackers, women used daggers and *naginata* (see page 29). Some warlords had bands of armed women patrolling the grounds of their castles.

▲ When using dogs as target practice, the horsemen used blunt arrows. It was not their intention to kill the dogs.

50 In another type of target practice, mounted samurai fired arrows at targets fixed to poles. They rode along a course, and as they moved past a small wooden board they fired an arrow. There were three targets, and the archer only had three arrows. The most skilful samurai made each arrow count and hit each target.

▶ Tomoe Gozen (c. 1157–1247) was a female warrior who fought on the side of the Minamoto clan during the Gempei War.

27

Weapons with edges

Hilt or handle
(*tsuka*)

52 Swords were the main edge weapons used by samurai. The blades were made of steel, in a process that involved heating and folding the metal several times. A sword was seen as the "soul" of a samurai. The finest swords were made by master swordsmiths. They carved their own names, the names of the owners, and good luck verses on the sword handles.

53 New swords were tested for sharpness. They were tried out on sheaves of straw wrapped around bamboo, oak poles, copper plates and even metal helmets. Sometimes they were tested on people too, and were used to behead criminals. The best swords were so sharp they could cut through several bodies placed on top of one another.

► A master swordsmith at work. Each time the steel was reshaped, the sword became stronger.

Scabbard (*saya*)

Guard (*tsuba*)

Point of blade (*kissaki*)

54
The main fighting sword was called a *katana*. It had a long, curving blade and was mainly used for combat on foot. The samurai held his sword in both hands as he moved it in a series of attacking strokes, from zigzags and circles to up, down and diagonal slashes. He could also use it on horseback, holding it with one hand, not two.

▲ Each *katana* was highly prized. The best swords were given names, such as "The Monster Cutter" or "Little Dragon."

▲ Guards at the end of the hilt (handle) of a *katana* stopped the swordsman's hand from slipping onto the blade.

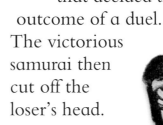

▲ A short sword or *tanto* and its scabbard. Like the *katana*, the *tanto* was incredibly sharp.

◄ The curved blade at the end of a *naginata*.

55
Short swords called *tanto* were used for fighting at close quarters. Every samurai carried a *tanto*. It was often the stabbing thrust of a *tanto* that decided the outcome of a duel. The victorious samurai then cut off the loser's head.

56
Samurai used other weapons with sharp edges. The *naginata* was a long pole with a curved metal blade at the end. The blade was used for slashing, and the pole for beating. It was mainly a weapon of the *ashigaru*, who also used stabbing spears.

► Most spears had pointed tips. Some were hook-shaped and used to drag men from their horses.

Missile weapons

57 **The bow was as important to the samurai as the sword.** It was called a *yumi*, and was almost 8 feet (2.5 meters) in length. Made from strips of wood and bamboo, it fired arrows to a distance of about 1,250 feet (380 meters), but its killing range was no more than about 260 feet (80 meters).

▶ Arrowheads came in different shapes and sizes to carry out different functions.

Armor-piercing arrowheads

58 **Arrows were made of bamboo, and there were many types of arrowhead.** Some made whistling noises, some had armor-piercing tips, and some had forked heads to cut through ropes. One legend says a samurai archer sank an enemy ship by firing an arrow through its hull below the waterline.

Whistling arrowhead

Forked arrowhead

Match (rope for burning)

◀ The longbow was an effective weapon, and samurai archers were highly trained.

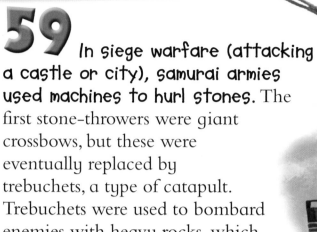

59

In siege warfare (attacking a castle or city), samurai armies used machines to hurl stones. The first stone-throwers were giant crossbows, but these were eventually replaced by trebuchets, a type of catapult. Trebuchets were used to bombard enemies with heavy rocks, which shattered when they hit the ground, causing casualties and damage.

▼ Samurai soldiers prepare to hurl a rock from a trebuchet.

▼ An *ashigaru* takes aim with an arquebus. Although these guns fired bullets in quick succession, they were less accurate than a skilled archer using a bow.

Barrel

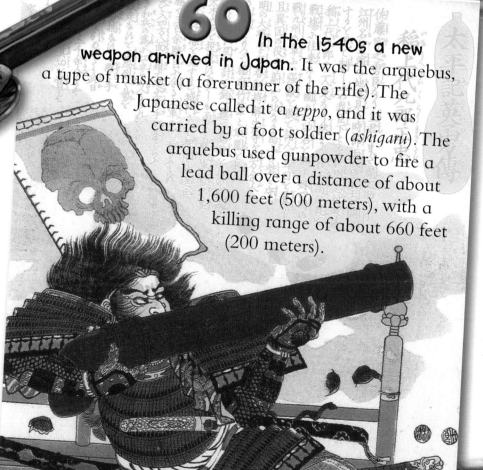

60

In the 1540s a new weapon arrived in Japan. It was the arquebus, a type of musket (a forerunner of the rifle). The Japanese called it a *teppo*, and it was carried by a foot soldier (*ashigaru*). The arquebus used gunpowder to fire a lead ball over a distance of about 1,600 feet (500 meters), with a killing range of about 660 feet (200 meters).

61

Another gunpowder weapon was the cannon. However, unlike the arquebus, which was widely used, the cannon was not very popular with samurai armies. Any cannon that were used came from Dutch and English ships that visited Japan.

◄ This soldier is using a large bore arquebus, which fired a big lead ball.

Amazing armor

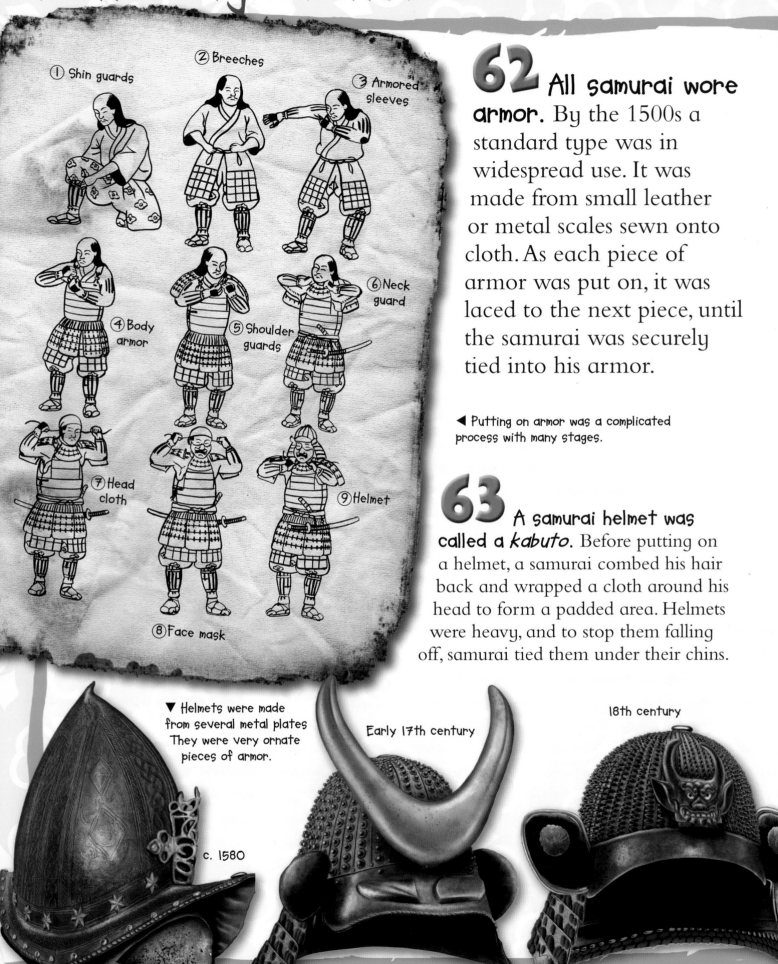

① Shin guards
② Breeches
③ Armored sleeves
④ Body armor
⑤ Shoulder guards
⑥ Neck guard
⑦ Head cloth
⑧ Face mask
⑨ Helmet

62 **All samurai wore armor.** By the 1500s a standard type was in widespread use. It was made from small leather or metal scales sewn onto cloth. As each piece of armor was put on, it was laced to the next piece, until the samurai was securely tied into his armor.

◀ Putting on armor was a complicated process with many stages.

63 **A samurai helmet was called a *kabuto*.** Before putting on a helmet, a samurai combed his hair back and wrapped a cloth around his head to form a padded area. Helmets were heavy, and to stop them falling off, samurai tied them under their chins.

▼ Helmets were made from several metal plates They were very ornate pieces of armor.

c. 1580

Early 17th century

18th century

64 Most samurai went into battle barefaced, but some wore a face mask, or *mempo*. This could cover the whole of the face, or just the chin, cheeks, mouth and nose. The mask was usually painted, and the mouth was shaped like a grimace so the warrior looked as if he was snarling.

▲ Some masks had bristling fake moustaches to make the wearer seem even more terrifying.

65 Samurai armor could be brightly colored. Lacquer (varnish) was painted over each piece. It not only made the armor stand out, it also made it hard-wearing. The five "lucky" colors were red, blue, yellow, black and white.

▶ Eighteenth-century armor from the Edo Period.

66 Samurai of the Li clan in the 1500s were known as the Red Devils. Their armor was coated with red lacquer, making them instantly recognizable. They chose red to make themselves appear more frightening, and because no other clan wore this color.

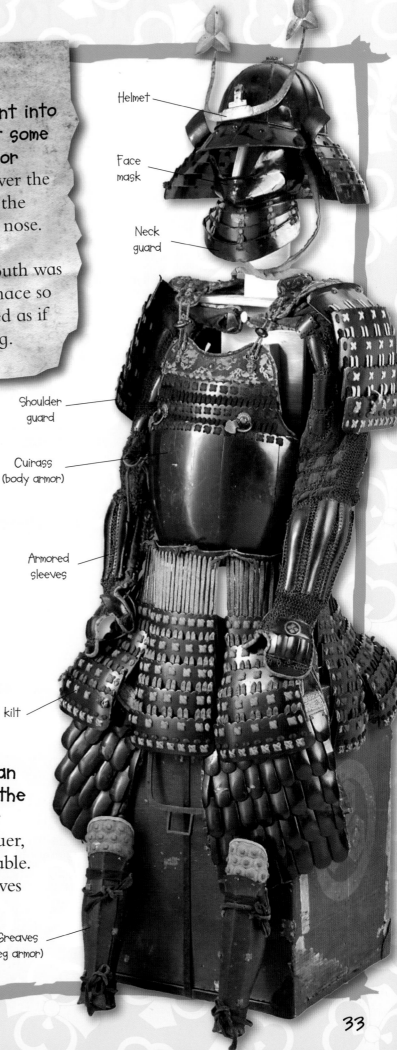

Helmet

Face mask

Neck guard

Shoulder guard

Cuirass (body armor)

Armored sleeves

Armored kilt

Greaves (leg armor)

Clothes and food

67 **For everyday clothing a samurai wore a *kimono*.** This was a long, wide-sleeved gown that came to below his knees and was kept in place by a belt wrapped around the waist. He wore a pair of *hakama* (wide trousers) under the *kimono* and socks and sandals on his feet. His *katana* (sword) was tucked into his belt.

Kimono

Katana

▶ A samurai in everyday dress. Even though he was not fighting, he still carried his sword.

Hakama

◀ A samurai with a typically shaven head. His remaining hair was tied in a bun at the back.

Socks and sandals

68 **Tidy hair was important.** It was considered a disgrace if a man let his hair become untidy. In the 1500s, samurai began shaving the hair from the front part of their heads. This made it more comfortable to wear a helmet in battle. Hair at the sides and rear of the head was combed back and tied into a bun.

I DON'T BELIEVE IT!

Tokugawa Ieyasu, leader of the Tokugawa clan in the 1500s, didn't like shaved heads—he said it spoiled the look of a head when it was cut off!

69 **Rice was the staple food in Japan.** It was eaten boiled and steamed, and as rice cakes and rice balls. Fish, pork, boar and rabbit were the main meats eaten. When samurai went to war, most warriors took portions of rice with them. If they raided an enemy camp or village, they took the enemy's food supplies.

◀ A local farmer offers a samurai commander baskets of melons for his troops. Fruit was popular with soldiers on campaign.

70 **Before a battle, samurai shared a meal together.** It was a way of bringing the warriors closer to each other in the last few hours before fighting began.

71 **A helmet was not just for wearing.** Some foot soldiers (*ashigaru*) used their metal helmets as cooking pots! They turned them upside down and boiled rice inside them over a fire. Small groups of men probably took it in turns to cook for their comrades.

▶ An *ashigaru*'s metal helmet had two functions—protective armor and a cooking pot to boil rice.

Castle fortresses

72 **To protect their territory, samurai clans built castles.** Some were built on flat plains, but most were built on mountains. Their purpose was to defend key areas such as bridges, river crossings, roads and mountain passes.

▶ A castle was surrounded by a strong wall. Inside were courtyards, each of which could be closed off if intruders broke through the main defenses.

73 **Castles built in the 1500s were heavily defended.** At the center was the keep—the tallest and grandest building within the castle grounds, where the *daimyo* (warlord) lived. If intruders broke through the castle's outer line of defense, they were faced by a series of walls with gates that took them into open courtyards—where they could be easily attacked.

I DON'T BELIEVE IT!

Tottori Castle was besieged for 200 days. The occupants ran out of food and had to eat grass, dead horses, and possibly even each other.

③

④

74 A clan's most important castle was the home of the *daimyo*. Around this castle were the homes of generals and family members. The more important the person was, the closer to the leader's castle they were allowed to live. A town grew up around the castle. Rice was grown in the surrounding fields to provide food for the townspeople.

75 Matsumoto Castle is one of Japan's finest samurai castles. It was built in the late 1500s, on a flat plain in central Japan. Its location made it an easy target, but the builders protected it with three moats and strong ramparts. The castle complex was surrounded by an earth wall 2.2 miles (3.5 kilometers) in circumference. The only way to enter or leave was through two heavily fortified gates.

76 Castles were difficult to attack. Armies besieged a castle until its occupants surrendered. When Takamatsu Castle was besieged in 1582, the attackers diverted a river until it formed a lake. As the lake grew, it flooded the castle, and the occupants gave in. The defeated leader rowed out on the lake and committed suicide (*seppuku*).

KEY
1. Keep (where the *daimyo* lived)
2. Moat
3. Outer wall
4. Inner wall
5. Gatehouse

The age of battles

77 Many battles took place all over Japan in the years 1450–1600. This time is known as the Warring States Period. It was a time of civil war, when rival states attacked each other, trying to win territory. The battles were fought on a large scale, and from the mid-16th century arquebuses were used—the first time this deadly firearm was put into practice in a big way.

78 Armies fought in battle formations. Generals decided which formation was best to use, and the troops moved into place. Formations had names such as "birds in flight," "keyhole," and "half moon." In the "birds in flight" formation, the arquebusiers protected the archers, who fired arrows over the heads of the musketmen. The general was at the center, surrounded by his warriors.

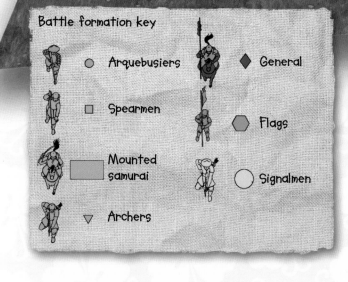

Battle formation key

Arquebusiers ● General ◆

Spearmen ■ Flags ⬡

Mounted samurai ▬ Signalmen ◯

Archers ▽

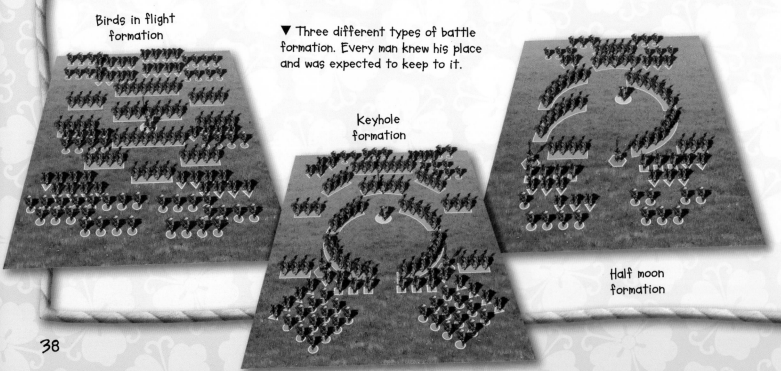

Birds in flight formation

▼ Three different types of battle formation. Every man knew his place and was expected to keep to it.

Keyhole formation

Half moon formation

79 The "arrowhead" formation was used to break through enemy lines. Arquebusiers fired their muskets, opening up gaps in the enemy's front ranks. When the gaps were big enough, samurai rushed past their gunmen, and through the gaps. Hand-to-hand fighting followed using swords, daggers, *naginata* and spears.

◄ The arrowhead formation takes its name from the pointed arrow-like position of the troops.

80 After the battle, the victors took the spoils. The dead of both sides were stripped of their weapons and armor. Scavengers from nearby villages helped themselves to whatever they could carry. Wounded warriors were of no use to anyone. They were killed by local villagers, who then took their belongings.

81 The greatest prizes were the heads of the losers. They were cut off and presented to the general for him to inspect. First, the heads were washed, the hair was combed, and they were placed on spikes on boards. Labels attached to the hair gave the names of the dead, and the names of the men who had killed them.

▼ The severed head of an enemy soldier being presented for inspection.

I DON'T BELIEVE IT!

If the eyes of a severed head were closed, it was a lucky sign. If they were open and looking upward, it was an unlucky sign.

Oda Nobunaga

82 **One of greatest samurai commanders of the Warring States Period was Oda Nobunaga.** He was born in 1534, and became *daimyo* (warlord) of the Oda clan when he was just 16. Because he was so young, rival clans thought they could easily overpower his army and take his land —but they were wrong. In a series of battles, Nobunaga's forces defeated his enemies.

84 **The Battle of Nagashino was fought in 1575.** In this great battle, Nobunaga sent an army to the castle of Nagashino. The castle was besieged by an army from the Takeda clan. Nobunaga's plan was to end the siege by fighting the Takedas.

83 **Nobunaga's rise to power began in 1560.** In that year, his territory was invaded by the Imagawa clan. The Imagawa army was 12 times the size of Nobunaga's, and they quickly took several of his fortresses. It looked as if Nobunaga would be defeated. But, during a thunderstorm, Nobunaga mounted a surprise attack. The Imagawa *daimyo* was killed, and Nobunaga's territory was saved.

▶ Japanese artists portrayed Oda Nobunaga as a fearsome warrior.

85

85 The Nobunaga and Takeda armies clashed on a plain near Nagashino Castle. Mounted samurai from the Takeda clan charged at Nobunaga's forces, and were felled by shots from as many as 3,000 arquebusiers. A second wave of Takeda horsemen swooped down, by which time the musketmen had reloaded. After hours of bitter fighting, the Takeda army withdrew.

QUIZ

1. How old was Nobunaga when he became leader of his clan?
2. What was the weather like when Nobunaga defeated the Imagawa daimyo?
3. How many arquebusiers did Nobunaga use against the Takedas?
4. When was the Battle of Nagashino?
5. In which city did Nobunaga die?

Answers:
1. 16 2. There was a thunderstorm 3. 3,000 4. 1575 5. Kyoto

▼ A scene from *Kagemusha*, a film released in 1980. Set during the Warring States Period, it ends with the Battle of Nagashino.

86 Oda Nobunaga died in 1582. He had become the most powerful general in Japan, and acted as if he was the country's shogun. This made him many enemies. On a visit to Honnoji Temple, in Kyoto, he was attacked by his own men. Some accounts say he died in the attack, others say he was captured and forced to commit *seppuku*.

Flags and standards

87 Samurai carried flags and standards into battle. There could be hundreds of flags fluttering in the wind on the battlefield, and each one had its own meaning. Some were decorated with family, clan or religious symbols, others had messages on them. It was the job of an army's foot soldiers to carry the flags.

88 A battlefield could be a confusing place. In the rush of horses and the scattering of men, it was easy for a soldier to become separated from his fellow warriors, or lose sight of his *daimyo* (warlord). If this happened, all he had to do was look around for the flags of his own side, which he recognized by their familiar symbols.

▲ The Soma-Nomaoi Festival is held each year in Haramachi City. Here, horsemen in traditional samurai armor parade with flags decorated with clan symbols, or *mons*.

▼ ▶ The red umbrella great standard of Oda Nobunaga and the golden bell great standard of Mukai Tadakatsu, leader of the Omura clan.

89 In samurai battles of the late 1500s and 1600s, the *daimyo* had two standards. They were the "great standard" and the "lesser standard," both were mounted on long poles. A standard was an important object to a clan. Not only was it instantly recognizable, it represented what the clan stood for, and was to be protected.

91 **Samurai could attach flags to their backs.** These were called *sashimono*. The shaft of the flag slotted into a holder in the armor, leaving both hands free for weapons. *Sashimono* were often decorated with the clan's colors or symbols. Some samurai painted their flags with messages, giving the name of the wearer and the name of the man he hoped to kill in battle.

▶ A *sashimono* attached to the back of a samurai. "Leader" is written on his flag in Japanese.

90 **It was a great honor to be a standard-bearer, but this honor brought danger.** The enemy was drawn toward the other side's standard, so the standard-bearer was always in the thick of the fighting. The defending army would do everything they could to save the standard from being captured. If the standard-bearer fell, another man quickly took his place.

DESIGN A FLAG

Have a close look at the flags pictured in this book, then design one of your own. Note how the flags are long and thin, which made them easy to carry. Keep your design simple and bold, and use strong colors so that it really stands out.

43

Samurai in decline

► Tokugawa Ieyasu, the shogun who brought a long period of peace to Japan.

92 **On October 21, 1600, the Battle of Sekigahara took place.** It was fought between the armies of Tokugawa Ieyasu (with 80,000 men) and Ishida Mitsunari (100,000 men). An estimated 30,000 men died on the battlefield. The Tokugawa clan won, and the battle brought an end to the Warring States Period.

93 **Tokugawa Ieyasu became shogun in 1603.** It was the start of a relatively peaceful period in Japan's history that lasted for the next 250 years. In 1639, Japan became a "closed country." It was forbidden to have contact with foreigners, and Japanese people were not even allowed to leave the country.

▼ The arrival of the American navy in Tokyo harbor in 1853 caused great concern in Japan.

▼ Emperor Meiji ruled Japan from 1868 to 1912.

94 **The clans were now at peace with each other, and their armies were disbanded.** The idea of going to war to steal another clan's territory became a thing of the past. Samurai traditions and rituals still carried on, but they were performed for peaceful purposes.

95 **In 1853 and 1854, a fleet of ships from the U.S.A. arrived in Tokyo Harbor.** The American fleet was led by Commodore Matthew Perry. His aim was for Japan to stop being a closed country and to open up to foreign trade. The Tokugawa clan were still Japan's rulers, and the shogun Tokugawa Iesada decided to open up the country. Many Japanese thought this was a bad thing.

96 **Japan's system of an emperor sharing power with the shogun came to an end in 1867.** It was a system that had lasted for 675 years. The last shogun, Tokugawa Yoshinobu, handed power back in 1867, and in 1868, Emperor Meiji became the sole ruler of Japan. For some people, these changes were too much to bear.

The last samurai

97 **The Satsuma Rebellion took place in 1877.** Samurai were unhappy at the changes in Japan. For centuries they had been respected, and feared, members of society. Gradually their way of living had changed, and now they felt out of place as Japan began a process of modernization, bringing to an end centuries of feudal rule. When they were told to lay down their swords, it was the final insult, and a rebellion began.

▶ Saigo Takamori (1828–1877), leader of the rebel forces during the Satsuma Rebellion, was the last samurai commander.

▲ Soldiers of the Japanese army with rifles (left) clash with samurai armed with *naginata*.

98 **Leader of the rebellion was Saigo Takamori.** His army of 40,000 samurai fought against a larger government force. The samurai fought with their traditional weapons—the sword and the bow. The Japanese army fought with rifles.

99 **The rebellion lasted for about eight months.** It ended at the Battle of Shiroyama, on September 24, 1877. Takamori's forces had been reduced to a few hundred men. He was heavily outnumbered, but refused to surrender as this was against the *bushido* code. Takamori was wounded, and then he committed *seppuku* rather than face being captured. His remaining men were cut down by gun fire.

100 **Many films have been made about the samurai.** The most famous is *Seven Samurai*, made in Japan in 1954 and set in the Warring States Period. Another is *Kagemusha*, made in 1980. Both of these films were directed by Akira Kurosawa, who is regarded as the greatest samurai film-maker of all time. Hollywood has also made films about samurai, such as *The Last Samurai* in 2003 with Tom Cruise in the title role.

▼ In the 2003 Warner Brothers' film *The Last Samurai*, actor Tom Cruise plays the part of an American fighting on the side of the samurai during the Satsuma Rebellion.

I DON'T BELIEVE IT!

In the *Star Wars* movies, the costume of Darth Vader was inspired by samurai armor.

Index

Entries in **bold** refer to main subject entries. Entries in *italics* refer to illustrations.